Original title:
Garden of Odes

Copyright © 2025 Creative Arts Management OÜ
All rights reserved.

Author: Mariana Leclair
ISBN HARDBACK: 978-1-80566-623-3
ISBN PAPERBACK: 978-1-80566-908-1

Stanzas Beneath the Stars

Under the night, the crickets sing,
While frogs in tuxedos dance and swing.
The moon winks bright with a big grin,
Counting the laughs of all the kin.

The stars, they throw a cosmic show,
As raccoons play tag with a wild doe.
A silver comet trips on a cloud,
And laughter echoes, merry and loud.

The Quiet Corners

In corners where the daisies peek,
A squirrel wears glasses, all unique.
He reads a book titled, 'How to Chill',
While ladybugs plan a dance on the hill.

A cactus wears hats, oh what a sight,
It hosts a party every night.
With buzzing bees serving tea so sweet,
And ants doing pirouettes on tiny feet.

Vibrations of the Vineyard

In the vineyard, the grapevines sway,
Mice play music, while squirrels ballet.
The sun spills juice on the clumsy grapes,
Turning them into funny shapes.

The wind whirls round with a silly tune,
As llamas try out for a dance with the moon.
They trip on vines, the laughter flows,
Creating a festival as the evening glows.

Whims of the Windflower

The windflower twirls with a playful swoop,
Inviting butterflies for a silly loop.
They tumble and spin, like popcorn in air,
While bumblebees sport their new rubber hair.

With petals that giggle, they take a spin,
Creating a ruckus, let the fun begin!
The sun rolls its eyes at the wild affair,
As laughter dances through the fragrant air.

Moonlit Reveries

In shadows deep where crickets sing,
A squirrel wears a tiny ring.
He dances round the garden bed,
With acorns stuffed right in his head.

The moonlight spills, a silver brew,
While frogs hop in a ballet too.
The flowers giggle, what a sight,
As night unfolds in sheer delight.

Beneath the Canopy of Color

A butterfly with glasses bold,
Claims it saw a worm named Gold.
They swap some jokes, oh what a mess,
The worm just can't wear that dress!

The daisies sway and whisper loud,
Discussing plans to form a crowd.
A dandelion spills some seeds,
Like confetti for funny deeds.

Petals in the Breeze

A petal fights the windy tease,
It twirls around with silly ease.
A bumblebee buzzes, 'Hey, that's mine!'
While roses blush and sip on wine.

The butterflies play tag in flight,
While sunflowers join in the delight.
But bees bring news, they can't believe,
The tulips are now wearing leaves!

The Enchanted Veil of Silences

A snail in armor takes a stroll,
He claims he's searching for a goal.
But really, he just wants some snacks,
And might forget the way he packs.

The wise old owl, with glasses round,
Snores softly in the branches sound.
The crickets laugh at all his dreams,
For silence is filled with giggly schemes.

The Rhythm of Growth

In the patch where veggies dance,
A tomato slips, a clumsy prance.
Chasing chickens, oh what a sight,
Cucumbers chuckle, just full of delight.

Beets wear hats and wiggle low,
While carrots gossip, putting on a show.
Each leaf a laugh, each root a cheer,
In this quirky plot, joy grows near.

Songs Carried by the Wind

The daisies hum a silly tune,
As butterflies wear capes under the moon.
A bumblebee buzzes, oh so proud,
Telling jokes to a giggling cloud.

The breeze plays tricks with petals bright,
Sending daisies into a dizzy flight.
With every gust, chuckles unfold,
Nature's humor, a sight to behold.

Trill of the Unseen

In this patch, the critters jest,
A snail plays piano, doing its best.
The ants go marching, sing a fun tune,
While worms do ballet beneath the moon.

Frogs croak comedy, they've got flair,
While grasshoppers leap with a wild air.
Invisible giggles from roots below,
Reveal the laughter in nature's show.

Portrait of a Forgotten Path

Where daisies argue with weeds in style,
A path lies hidden, not traveled for a while.
Gnomes shake heads, sharing tales of yore,
While squirrels debate what nuts are for.

Mossy stones hold secrets of cheer,
As lizards act like they own the frontier.
Each twist and turn, a comic parade,
A whimsical map where joy is laid.

A Tapestry of Bloom

In a patch of daisies, a bee does prance,
Wearing tiny shades, he thinks he can dance.
A butterfly flutters, with flair so grand,
But trips on a petal and lands in the sand.

The tulips gossip with a giggling sound,
"Did you see that bee? He's the talk of the town!"
With colors so bright, they strut and they pose,
While the daisies roll laughter, their heads full of woes.

Echoes of Greenery

The carrots debate who's the best in the patch,
While the peas cast their votes but scratch their heads,
quite a batch.
A gnome overhears, with a wink and a grin,
And he chuckles aloud, "Come on, let's begin!"

The tomatoes blush red, feeling quite rare,
While the lettuce turns crisp in the sunny affair.
As the radishes giggle, all merry and bright,
Claiming they're the stars of the day and the night.

Melodies Among the Vines

The grapevines sing songs of their juicy delight,
While squirrels hold concerts, much to their fright.
A rabbit comes hopping, with carrots to share,
But stumbles in rhythm, causing quite a scare!

The cucumbers sway, with a rhythmic obsession,
As the tomatoes roll by in a quiet procession.
With laughter erupting, from root to the shoot,
Even the daisies join with a flute and a toot!

Symphony of Sunlight

The sunbeams do tango across leafy floors,
While shadows jabber about garden lore.
A worm in a hat starts to wiggle and twist,
Singing, "I'm the star, you just can't resist!"

The daisies all blush as the sunlight does glint,
Swapping tall tales, over tea they imprint.
And while they all chuckle, with petals so fair,
Even the weeds join in, twirling without a care.

Serenades of the Soil

In the dirt, worms like to wiggle,
While plants laugh and giggle.
A potato wears a crown so bright,
Claiming it's a vegetable knight.

Sunflowers gossip in the breeze,
Telling tales with such ease.
Bees dance like they own the place,
Buzzing round with silly grace.

A carrot dreams of being sweet,
But gets lost where the stinky feet.
Radishes wear big red caps,
Throwing parties with all their chaps.

Soil sings a tune, oh so sly,
With each sprout saying, 'Give it a try!'
In this earthy, zany sprawl,
Nature cracks jokes—the best of all!

The Breath of Blossoms

Daisies flaunt their sunny smiles,
While tulips strut around in styles.
Petunias giggle and sway with flair,
As roses blush, caught in mid-air.

A daffodil trips over a bee,
Bumbling round, as it tries to flee.
Lilies play peek-a-boo with the sun,
While chatting about their day's fun.

Violets whisper secrets, oh so sly,
While pansies ponder life—oh why?
A clover believes it's lucky, you see,
And jests around like it's hosting tea.

With colors bright, they steal the scene,
In this wild display, nothing routine.
Hilarity blooms where fragrance roams,
In fragrant fields, here laughter homes!

Chronicles of the Canopy

Up in the branches, squirrels convene,
Playing tag, the cheeky routine.
Leaves rustle secrets, birds hold court,
While ants parade in their tiny sort.

A raccoon juggles nuts with pride,
As wise old owls give wisdom wide.
The sunbeams laugh and twirl about,
Turning shadows into playful rout.

Caterpillars dream of wings to soar,
While beetles march, seeking to explore.
The canopy hums a forest tune,
With echoes of mischief from dawn till noon.

With every branch, a story spun,
In this leafy realm, there's never just one.
Nature's antics, a comical play,
Under the verdant, wild ballet!

The Radiance of Raindrops

Raindrops dance upon my nose,
Each one tickles, and then it goes.
Turn around, and oh what fun,
Jumping puddles, we can run.

Here comes splashes, big and small,
Honestly, it's a splash-tastic ball!
We kick our feet and laugh so loud,
Under the clouds, we feel so proud.

But umbrellas become our hats,
A fashion show? Just call the cats!
With giggles bursting, we can't stop,
Let's race the rivulets—oh, what a plop!

So grab your boots, don't be a bore,
Let's have some fun, who wants more?
Nature's laughter, such a delight,
In the radiant rain—what a sight!

Hymns of the Hearth

Gather 'round, it's hearth time, folks,
With warming tales and silly jokes.
Let's roast some marshmallows, take a bite,
While shadows dance in flickering light.

A cat's on the mantel, so full of sass,
Paws twitching at the warmth—oh, what a class!
But give it a nibble of the charred treat,
And you'll discover now who's elite!

The flames crackle like a giggling child,
And every spark makes the old world wild.
With stories shared, the night gets fun,
Laughter echoes, two-for-one!

So raise a toast, the evening is prime,
To hearth and home, let's sing in rhyme.
Through laughter and snacks, our night's complete,
In our cozy nook, nothing can't beat!

Reflections of the Rivulet

Mirror, mirror, on the stream,
Can you reflect my wildest dream?
Flip-flops float as ducks chase by,
Splashing water—I think I can fly!

The frogs croak tunes for our delight,
Crooning ballads into the night.
With stones we skip and try to boast,
But mostly we make a big wet toast!

Oh quick, look out for buzzing bees,
As they hum their tunes among the trees.
Our laughter tumbles, sweet and light,
While we chase shadows till the night.

Let's dive in deep and make some waves,
Call all the fishes and dive like brave knaves.
Rippling joy that shimmers so bright,
In our little stream, we take flight!

The Tethered Tansy

In a patch where tansy sways,
With laughter, we spend our days.
Dancing bees buzz near and far,
What a funny place we are!

Tansy twirls in a dizzy spree,
While we giggle at a bumblebee.
Oh watch it slip on garden shoes,
Then blame its pals for making a ruse!

With wildflowers all in play,
Dandelions laugh and sway away.
"Tickle my roots!" they shout with glee,
While petals rain down—are you with me?

So come, join the fun, don't be shy,
Let's frolic till the summer's nigh.
In our tangled patch, hearts take flight,
With tethered tansies, all feels right!

The Epiphany of Essence

In the patch where daisies dance,
The gnomes are caught in sweet romance.
A squirrel sneezes with such flair,
A cascade of acorns in mid-air!

Butterflies wear tiny hats,
While rabbits play cards with clever chats.
The tulips gossip in the breeze,
Tickling each other with secrets, please!

Symphony beneath the Sycamore

Under the tree with wide-set arms,
A troupe of ants shows off their charms.
They play their tunes on bits of leaves,
Creating a sound that truly deceives.

Crickets jump in a wild ballet,
As snails cheer in their own slow way.
The wind joins in, a jolly friend,
Together they sing, as daylight ends.

Traces of Tranquility

In a nook where humor grows,
A lazy cat in the sun doze.
He dreams of fish and the chase at night,
As butterflies swirl in glorious flight.

The flowers chuckle in vibrant hues,
While sleepy bees take their afternoon snooze.
The pond reflects a silly grin,
As frogs leap high, both out and in.

The Petal's Promise

Each petal swears it will not fade,
While critters play a sneaky charade.
A ladybug plans a wobbly trip,
But gets caught in a dewdrop's grip!

The winking daisies start a race,
Against the wind, they quicken their pace.
Amidst the chaos, laughter erupts,
As playful shadows joyfully disrupts!

The Language of Leaves

In whispers soft, the leaves do talk,
They gossip more than busy folk.
They giggle when the breezes tease,
And dance around like buzzing bees.

The oak gave me a secret wink,
The willow sighed, 'Oh, what a brink!'
Maples blush when sunlight's bold,
While pines just pine for tales retold.

Each rustling word a playful jest,
A leafy joke, the very best!
So if you stroll beneath their shade,
Join in their laughs, don't be afraid!

From every branch, a jest does sprout,
The leaves declare, 'Come, dance about!'
In this leafy realm, let laughter flow,
For joy is found where green things grow.

Ode to the Hidden Nook

In corners deep where sunlight hides,
A cozy spot where mischief glides.
Small critters plot their grand escape,
While petals play a sneaky shape.

The shadows whisper jokes so sly,
And clouds above just pass on by.
Here ants parade with tiny hats,
While ladybugs discuss their spats.

Forget me not and dandelions,
They group together, forming pines.
Their laughter bounces 'round the bends,
A place where silliness transcends.

So if you find this hidden nook,
Just stop and take a silly look.
For in this realm, the laughter croons,
Where every glance brings forth cartoons.

The Dance of the Daisies

Oh daisies twirl in sunshine's ray,
In flowery skirts, they lead the ballet.
With petals pointed, they can't resist,
The urge to dance, they simply insist!

They twirl and spin, a floral spree,
In every gust, they cheer with glee.
Grass blades sway, they join the flow,
A merry party, putting on a show.

Hummingbirds laugh at their delight,
While butterflies flutter in the light.
Each flower's wiggle is pure sweet glee,
A dancing floor for all to see.

So join the fun, you're welcome too,
The daisies say, "We'll dance with you!"
In this riot of colors, take a chance,
And let your spirit join the dance!

Soliloquy in the Wildflowers

In wildflowers bold, a speech begins,
Where daisies mock and thistles grin.
Each blossom stands a stage so grand,
With petals bright, their laughter planned.

A tulip cried, "Oh, look at me!"
While daisies rolled in jubilee.
The poppies teased with cheeky flair,
"Oh, who wears red? Come on, beware!"

A daffodil then took the lead,
With puns and jests, she dared to plead.
"Join in our tale, let laughter soar,
There's plenty here, and then some more!"

In this bright thicket, joy does reign,
Each petal's phrase a sweet champagne.
So stop and hear their silly tunes,
For nature's humor brightens the moons.

Chronicles of the Wild Blooms

In a patch of sunlight, flowers giggle,
Bees buzzing tunes, as they wiggle.
A dandelion wears sunglasses cool,
While violets vote to skip school.

Tulips in tutus, dance on the breeze,
Caterpillars wear fancy, patchy fleece.
A rose tells jokes, prickles aside,
While pansies giggle until they cried.

Sunflowers bask in warm daylight,
Telling tall tales of the moonlight.
Snapdragons snap with sarcastic flare,
While the lilies lounge without a care.

The daisies play cards, they cheat and bluff,
While petunias argue about the tough stuff.
Each cheeky bloom has a secret to share,
In the wild blooms' world, there's laughter everywhere.

Whispers of Blossoms

Amidst the blooms, whispers doth roam,
A daisy declared, "I'm taking a comb!"
The marigold chuckled, adjusting its curls,
As lavender twirled in her purple pearls.

Pansies gossip about sneezy bees,
"Why can't they learn to say, 'Excuse me, please?'"
The tulips pranced, too proud to care,
As daisies snorted, "What a bright affair!"

Violets wager on who blooms first,
While peonies argue, their style is cursed.
A sunflower rolls its eyes so high,
"Can't we all agree? Let's just get by!"

Beside the paths, the thyme sips tea,
With the rosemary laugh, "Who's next to flee?"
In this blossom world, where sprightly dance,
Laughter sprinkles like petals in chance.

Serenade of Petals

A chorus of flora sings soft and loud,
"Look at me! I'm so lovely and proud!"
The pansies wink with a sly little grin,
While the sunflowers bask and soak up the din.

Petunias puff up, showing their might,
"Watch my colors bloom, oh what a sight!"
Daffodils joke, playing hide and seek,
"Why did the rose skip? It needed a tweak!"

At dusk, they gather beneath the moon,
Chatting about flies that drone a tune.
The softest petals share tales of woe,
While violets tease, "Watch how I glow!"

In this patch of mirth, where laughter swells,
Each fragrant bloom has its own silly spells.
With giggles a-twinkle under the stars,
The serenade continues, no matter how far.

The Secret Orchard

In a hidden nook where whispers collide,
Fruits chuckle lightly, unable to hide.
"Why are the apples always so round?"
"Because we're the sweetest in this whole town!"

The cherries gossip, so bright and fair,
Wondering if bananas beware.
"Let's throw a party!" a plum exclaims,
"I'll bring the jokes, you bring the games!"

Peaches plot schemes, quite juicy and bold,
While oranges roll tales that never get old.
A fig with a wink says, "What's your plan?
Let's make this orchard the best in the land!"

With giggles resounding among the trees,
The veggies debate who has the best cheese.
In this secret place of frivolous mirth,
The orchard blooms tales of joy and rebirth.

Elysian Echoes

In a patch of greens, the gnomes do dance,
Beneath the sun's rays, they take a chance.
With cheeky grins and tiny hats,
They've formed a band with four green rats.

Chasing daisies, they slip and slide,
While bees form bands, all buzzing wide.
A flower throws shade, a petal's embrace,
As laughter erupts in this silly place.

Puddles provide a splashy stage,
Each drop a giggle, they're truly dazed.
A snail's slow waltz, so full of style,
Makes even the sun stop for a while.

So in this realm, where fun is found,
The echoes ripple, all around.
In every breeze, a chuckle's born,
Among the flora, we laugh 'til morn.

The Harmony of Hummingbirds

Hummingbirds zoom with zesty flair,
In tiny tutus, they don't care.
Flitting and fluttering through the blooms,
Creating chaos, it's all their tunes.

One sips nectar, wearing shades of blue,
Another's humming humor, just for you.
They chirp in chorus, a comic show,
While petals giggle, putting on a glow.

With every flutter, a giggle flies,
As flowers sway under the sunny skies.
The sunbeams join in, tap dancing bright,
In this wild party, pure delight.

So gather around for the jesters' flight,
With heart-shaped wings, they dance in light.
In their world of whimsy, join the cheer,
For laughter blooms in every year.

Verses of the Verdure

In the shade of leaves, the veggies plot,
Goofy grapevines twist, they're quite the lot.
Tomatoes tumble, giggling loud,
As carrots wear crowns, feeling proud.

Over the fence, a rabbit peeks,
To check on the fun, he hops and squeaks.
While onions cry out a silly song,
As broccoli joins in, where they belong.

Pansies chuckle, their colors bright,
As squash play tag under moon's soft light.
The radishes rave, red faces aglow,
While spinach sits back, taking it slow.

So in this patch where laughter reigns,
The green brigade is free from chains.
With every sprout, a joke is shared,
In this verdant realm, we're all prepared.

The Silk of Sunbeams

Sunbeams drape in golden threads,
They twirl around, tickling heads.
With every glint, a wink is tossed,
In the light's embrace, no joy is lost.

A daisy drops its petals like confetti,
While shadows sway, feeling quite yeti.
The sun laughs loud, a cheeky show,
As frogs join in with a croaky 'hello!'

Butterflies flutter, they wear a grin,
As flowers gossip, oh where to begin?
Each petal spins tales of their days,
In this realm of light, it's all a blaze.

So dance with the beams, let laughter flow,
As sunlit giggles put on a show.
In this tapestry spun by cheer,
Life blooms brighter when joy is near.

Chants of the Cacti

In the desert sun, they stand so tall,
Prickly but wise, they giggle and sprawl.
Needles for jokes, they poke at the breeze,
Sharing their puns with the bees and the trees.

When rain drops down, they dance with glee,
'We've finally scored, let's throw a spree!'
But when it pours, they wear a frown,
'Why can't it rain candy? Let's ditch this gown!'

The lizards laugh while the cacti boast,
'We're just too cool for the average host!'
With roots that wiggle and smiles that shine,
They're the weirdest party, and it's simply divine.

So here's a toast to the spiky crew,
Who find joy in the strangest of dew.
In their prickly world, the laughter is bright,
A comedy show under the moonlight.

Stories Spun in Silk

Silken threads dance in the warm morning light,
Spiders weave tales that twinkle just right.
With a flip and a spin, they share silly lore,
Of ants on a picnic and how to encore.

Each story grows longer, each yarn takes a twist,
Be careful, my friend, you might get the gist!
Of flower fairies in highflying boots,
Whispering secrets to the bumblebee flutes.

The night doesn't darken; it twinkles with fun,
As critters gather to bask in the sun.
Each tale ends in laughter, a giggling spree,
As silk threads unite for a grand jubilee.

So come one, come all, to this party of hue,
Where stories are spun in the garden's soft dew.
With every soft whisper, hearts joyfully swell,
In this world of wonder, where friendship is well.

The Fiesta of Flora

Petals and leaves join a dazzling dance,
A fiesta of colors at first glance.
Sunflowers swagger with hats on their heads,
While daisies gossip in their floral beds.

The roses start laughing, 'We're beautiful, see?'
But violets wink, 'We play hide and seek!'
With marigolds giggling and tulips in tune,
This floral fiesta is over the moon.

The bees buzz along, joining in on the fun,
'The nectar is sweet, come on, everyone!'
With each whirling bloom and fluttering wing,
They throw in some joy and start to sing.

So let's raise a glass to this colorful spree,
Where plants are the dancers, wild and free.
In this festival of laughter, oh what a sight,
Nature's grand theatre under the moonlight.

The Language of Living Things

In whispers and giggles, the vines share their glee,
With roots deep in soil, they chat endlessly.
'The sun's quite a joker, he tickles our leaves,'
Said the shy little sprout, 'It's hard to believe!'

The flowers all nod, 'What a silly day!
The grass is the punchline; it sways and it plays!'
With each rustling petal, a secret is told,
Of winds that are moody and sunlight like gold.

Butterflies flutter and join in the chat,
'Have you heard the latest? A mouse wore a hat!'
As crickets chime in on the night's funny scheme,
They craft silly jokes like they're living a dream.

So here's to the voices, both large and small,
The language of living things, connects us all.
In this whimsical world, where laughter takes wing,
Every creature is special and ready to sing.

The Weaver's Whisper

In the patch where daisies dance,
Threads of laughter twirl and prance.
A spider spins its web of dreams,
While bees buzz jokes in sunny beams.

The gnomes play cards under the trees,
Chasing squirrels with awkward ease.
A rabbit juggles carrots, quite a sight,
As butterflies cheer, soaring in delight.

The sun winks down with rays of fun,
Tickling petals, one by one.
A snail shouts, 'Race you to the fence!'
But moves at a pace that's quite intense!

The flowers gossip, petals a-flutter,
'Have you heard? The worms make butter!'
In this realm where giggles reign,
Every creature knows the joy of gain.

Muses of the Moonlit Blooms

At twilight's peek, the blossoms grin,
With petals soft, and giggles thin.
Owl recites a cheesy rhyme,
While fireflies light the stage sublime.

The roses tease the prickly thorns,
'Your jokes are sharp, but we're reborn!'
Laughter echoes by the sleepy pond,
As frogs in tuxedos sing and respond.

The mint leaves slip in moonlit beams,
'We stir up drinks and foolish dreams!'
And dandelions float, just like wishes,
While picking up giggles as soft as kisses.

In this night where mischief sways,
Every bloom blooms in funny ways.
As petals hold their secrets tight,
Laughter grows until the morning light.

Secrets of the Soft Earth

Beneath the ground, the critters plot,
With secrets shared that time forgot.
A worm recites its favorite book,
While moles devise a new cookbook.

The earthworms wiggle to a tune,
Dancing under the watchful moon.
A stone's rolled out to join the crew,
Saying, 'Dirt can be fun! Who knew?'

The ants debate the best of crumbs,
While sniffing out their giggly drums.
A root sprout sways, singing loud,
'Beneath the dirt, I'm very proud!'

With every turn of shovel and spade,
A raucous party gets well laid.
In cozy depths where laughter brews,
The soft earth hums its joyful blues.

Kaleidoscope of Colors

A rainbow spills upon the ground,
Where silly flowers meet, astound.
The red blooms shout, 'We're top-notch!'
While yellows giggle, 'Grab the Scotch!'

The blues compete in blooming style,
With violets who flirt and smile.
Orange zinnias sing out loud,
Holding court with a laughing crowd.

Petunias spin in wild ballet,
As greens hum tunes in sweet parlay.
The butterflies wear colorful frowns,
Moping 'bout upside-down crowns.

In this bright patch, mischief swirls,
Where every hue hops and twirls.
A vibrant world, all funny and bright,
Colors unite in pure delight.

The Verse of the Violets

In the corner, violets grin,
Wearing hats that spin and spin.
They gossip low, about the sun,
And dance around, just having fun.

A bee rolls by, he paints a scene,
With pollen wings, all bright and green.
He bumps a petal, calls her 'Sweet',
And then they share a buzzing treat.

The raindrops laugh, they drip and drop,
While petals giggle with each plop.
They whisper tales, of muddy shoes,
And how to win at hide and snooze.

But when the dusk begins to fall,
The violets gather, one and all.
They sing their song, in tones so loud,
A chorus proud, beneath the cloud.

Legacies of Lavender

In fields where lavender does play,
They twirl and twist, come what may.
With scents so sweet, they hold their ground,
While bees buzz loud, a funky sound.

A ladybug, in shades of red,
Claims every petal as her bed.
She dreams of castles, tall and wide,
And hosts a tea party inside.

The nightingale, with voice so bright,
Tries to croon a lullaby right.
But lavender shouts, "Not on our watch!"
"We're too busy swirling, you big botch!"

They flap their leaves, in silly dance,
And tease the wind to join their prance.
With every twirl, they share a laugh,
Oh, what a fragrant, silly half!

Shadows among the Shrubs

In shadows deep, the shrubs convene,
With all their whispers, calm and keen.
A raccoon joins, with snacks to share,
They swap old tales, without a care.

A squirrel struts, with acorns stacked,
He claims his prize, and we all act.
The bushes snicker, knowing well,
That acorns taste like tales to tell.

The shrubs join in, with leafy cheers,
Their roots entwined, as if to peer.
They cackle softly, 'round they go,
While shadows dance, putting on a show.

As twilight reels them into sleep,
They dream of pranks, not one too deep.
For in their world, full of jest,
Life is a game, and they're the best!

Tides of Time in a Trellis

Upon the trellis vines entwine,
They tell of love, that twists like wine.
With leaves that shimmer, bright and bold,
They share their secrets, funny, old.

A snail rolls by, in slow delight,
He claims to soar, on dreams of flight.
The vines just laugh, with gentle tease,
"Your slow-paced game? We'll take our leaves!"

The trellis creaks, it's wise and worn,
It mutters tales of love reborn.
And in the whimsy of each hour,
They sip on blossoms, oh, such power!

As sunsets paint the sky a scene,
The vines entwine, a leafy sheen.
They toast to time, both quick and slow,
In every twist, their laughter grows.

Wandering Through Flora's Heart

In a meadow full of blooms,
Flowers gossip, making zooms.
Daisies dance with all their might,
While roses blush, it's quite a sight.

Bees are buzzing, making sounds,
Flitting 'round like silly clowns.
Tulips tease the bumblebees,
"Catch us if you can, oh please!"

A sunflower tripped on its toes,
Fell into a patch of woes.
Laughter echoed, filled the air,
Nature's jesters everywhere!

With every petal's happy quirk,
The world laughs in its leafy work.
So I stroll through this delight,
Where every bloom ensures a laugh tonight.

The Canvas of Nature's Emotions

Brushes dipped in hues so bright,
Nature paints with sheer delight.
A daffodil in yellow dress,
Is surely feeling quite the mess.

Bluebells bloom in clusters bold,
Telling secrets still untold.
Every petal, every leaf,
Colors add to nature's grief.

The lavender wears scented crowns,
While ferns sport their leafy gowns.
Yet, the daisies roll on the ground,
Turning frowns to laughs all around.

Artful chaos, truly grand,
In this patchwork, nature planned.
A canvas vast with riddles spun,
Painting joy under the sun.

Hymn to the Soil

Oh soil beneath my happy feet,
You cradle seeds and make them sweet.
In your depths, they wiggle and play,
They pop up laughing, bright and gay.

Worms recite their squirmy tunes,
While ants march on like tiny loons.
Each scoop of earth holds giggles too,
As plants shout out, "We love you!"

Roots intertwine in puzzling ways,
Dancing together for endless days.
With every shovel, every dig,
The soil grins, it's rather big!

So here's to you, dear dirt and mud,
For every sprout, and every bud.
You're nature's stage for wild antics,
Where laughter blooms in all its antics.

Impressions of a Sunlit Dawn

At dawn, the sun spills golden light,
Tickling leaves with sheer delight.
Birds commence their morning jest,
Singing songs for nature's fest.

A squirrel hops from branch to branch,
With acorns hidden, just by chance.
He plops down with a funny squeak,
As petals blush, oh what a week!

Butterflies twirl in morning waltz,
While blooms erupt, nobody faults.
They whisper tales of wonderment,
In a realm that's rather bent.

So here we are, with sun-kissed glee,
Nature's laughter is all around me.
Each dawn renews the playful cheer,
With every bloom, the world is clear!

Ode to the Open Air

The breeze tickles my nose, a funny affair,
While a squirrel mocks me from a branch up there.
It wiggles its tail, a dance so absurd,
I laugh at my thoughts, feeling totally blurred.

A picnic spread wide, ants march like troops,
Stealing my sandwich; oh, such little stoops!
I wave my hands, a frantic ballet,
While they munch on my lunch, what can I say?

Bubbles of laughter float high in the sky,
Kites suddenly swoop, oh my, oh my!
With each gust of wind, mischief takes flight,
I chase my own hat, what a comical sight!

Beneath a bright sun, my worries take flight,
In this uproarious place, all feels just right.
With giggles and gaffes, my heart skips a beat,
This merriment here, oh, so light on my feet.

Journey Through Ferns

Wandering softly, I trip on a root,
Overgrown laughter in snug little boots.
The ferns wave at me, in a whimsical cheer,
"Don't mind us, friend, just swing your rear!"

Dancing with daisies, I start to prance,
A worm looks up, says, "Care for a dance?"
I teach him the twist, oh, what a delight,
He wiggles and giggles, we dance through the night.

A butterfly flutters, with flair, it takes wing,
And the bumblebees buzz, as if they can sing.
I join in their chorus, a comedic mime,
With my own little hum, I'm so out of rhyme!

In this whimsical kingdom, no frown to be found,
With every soft rustle, and each funny sound.
Through the ferns and the laughter, my heart feels so free,

In this frolicsome paradise, just nature and me.

Portrait of the Perennials

With a splash of color, the flowers all joke,
The daffodils giggle, and the tulips poke.
Each petal a grin, each stem a sly wink,
They whisper sweet secrets, oh, what do you think?

The sunflowers stand tall, thinking they're grand,
While clumsy bees buzz, completely unplanned.
"Hey, big guy!" we shout, "Don't block our good light!"
And the daisies all chuckle, "You're blocking our sight!"

The roses, so radiant, with a thorny sharp bite,
Married to humor, they giggle all night.
"Why so prickly?" I tease, with a wink in my eye,
"Just keeping it fresh!" they blush, oh my, oh my!

In this floral hilarity, I find my bright muse,
With blossoms so chatty, I can't help but amuse.
Their joy is contagious, their laughter pure gold,
In this floppy bouquet, we've stories untold.

The Rhythm of the Rain

Pitter-patter whispers, drops tap on the ground,
Plastic ducks laughing, wiggle around.
Umbrella in hand, I dance like a fool,
While puddles invite me to jump in their pool!

Laughter of raindrops, they chime a sweet tune,
With frogs conducting, under the full moon.
They ribbit and croak, in a slippery ballet,
I can't help but join in, it's the rain's kind of play!

My shoes are now soggy, squelching with glee,
Each splash sends me flying, oh look, that's a bee!
It hovers and darts, an aerial show,
While I leap and I laugh, with no place else to go.

So here in the downpour, I twirl and I spin,
In this drizzly delight, where the fun will begin.
With rain as my partner, we shimmy and sway,
Oh, the joy of wet dances – how silly, hooray!

Chronicles of the Climbing Roses

Once a rose climbed high on a wall,
Hoping one day it would be quite tall.
It slipped on a petal, oh what a sight,
Fell with a thud, quite the garden fright!

The daisies laughed, they giggled with glee,
"Roses don't fly, they stick to the tree!"
But up climbed the rose, spunky and bold,
Dreams of the sky made it brave and bold!

Thorns as its armor, it pushed back with zest,
Said, "I'm a climber, I won't be repressed!"
With a wink to the sun, it gave one last heave,
Now it winks at the clouds, oh, what a reprieve!

So in this green plot where we all plant our dreams,
Remember the roses and their funny schemes.
For laughter and petals make life oh so bright,
Even when you flub, you can still reach a height!

The Lullaby of Lilies

In a pond of tranquility, lilies rest,
Singing soft tunes, they feel quite blessed.
But a frog hopped by, with a great big croak,
Said, "Don't quit your day job! You're all just a joke!"

The lilies gasped, with petals a-flutter,
"How dare you, wise frog, with your rude little mutter?"
"We're singing perchance for the fishies to hear,
Not for a loud frog - shoo, my dear!"

But the frog just grinned, with a leap and a splash,
"Your lullabies fail, it's a silly old bash!"
With a twirl and a twist, the lilies they twinkled,
"Just watch and see if our melodies crinkled!"

So they sang through the night, and the stars had a laugh,
With each note they played, they felt quite the gaff.
In the still of the night, as the water did gleam,
Even frogs can't resist a good soggy dream.

Poems Written in Soil

Once there were poems, scribbled in dirt,
With words washed away, and a bit of hurt.
A worm wriggled by, with a chuckle so loud,
"These verses won't last, they're covered by cloud!"

"Oh, Mr. Worm, don't mock what you see,
For each word that's lost can sometimes still be!"
The daisies chimed in, sharing their cheer,
"In each little crumb, a story is here!"

But the wind picked up, swirled with more glee,
Tossing those poems like leaves in a spree.
The flowers all giggled, rolled on the ground,
"What fun to write things that can't be found!"

So if you find poems in the muck and the mire,
Remember it's laughter that lifts them so higher.
For in every lost verse, a secret might dwell,
Chasing the squirrel, or telling a snail!

Serenity Among the Shadows

In a patch of shadows where whispers reside,
Sat a cheeky gnome with a grand, goofy pride.
He wore a tall hat, way too big for his noggin,
Sipping on dew, as his imagination was joggin'!

"Oh, look at me! Just a gnome in a glade,
Making friends with the leaves, oh what a charade!"
He danced with the shadows, gave them a twirl,
While squirrels looked on, giving their best curl!

The flowers all giggled, the bees buzzed along,
As the gnome made up verses to his funny song.
"In this serene place, with shadows that play,
I'm the light-hearted jester, come join in the fray!"

So next time you're lost in a flickering grove,
Remember the gnome who found joy in the trove.
For laughter and light, whether dark or bright,
Are what make our hearts bloom, oh what a delight!

In the Embrace of Greenery

The daisies dance in silly glee,
While squirrels plot their next prank spree.
Roses giggle at the bugs that roam,
And butterflies claim this place as home.

Lettuce wears a hat so grand,
While onions chase the carrots; oh, how they planned!
Dandelions whisper secrets sweet,
As ants march on with tiny feet.

A snail slides by, a slow parade,
Declaring, 'Fast is just a charade!'
The sunbeams laugh with flecks of gold,
While shadows gossip tales retold.

The Hidden Realm of Blossoms

In the thicket, laughter rises,
From flowers wearing funny disguises.
Tulips boast of their fancy shoes,
While pansies cheer with playful views.

The bees are buzzin' tunes of grandeur,
While tickled petals share their candor.
Worms discuss their fancy dance,
While sunflowers give a hearty glance.

Gnomes play poker behind the boughs,
Counting blessings, and funny vows.
Every sprout a tale to tell,
In this realm where all is well.

Ode to the Timid Bud

Oh, tender bud, so shy and meek,
You hide away, refusing to speak.
With leaves that tremble in the breeze,
You blush, oh how you tease!

Your friends, the bold blooms, sing out loud,
While you huddle low beneath a cloud.
Like a child playing hide and seek,
You giggle softly, feeling unique.

But one fine morning, in the sun's warm glow,
You spread your petals, putting on a show.
Laughter rises from the cheerful throng,
As the timid bud finally joins the song.

Melodies from the Earth

A toad croaks tunes with a jazzy flair,
While crickets join with legs in the air.
The wind plays flute through branches wide,
And daisies sway in joyful stride.

A worm on a ukulele strums,
While tree frogs tap their tiny drums.
The grass hums softly as it sways,
In this orchestra of sunny days.

Even the rocks wear a tune so grand,
As the earth dances, hand in hand.
In this symphony of joyful mirth,
We find the sweetest songs of earth.

Rhapsody of Roots

Amidst the soil, the carrots dream,
A beetroot's blush outshines the cream.
The radishes dance with leafy flair,
While peas gossip about the air.

The tomatoes giggle in the sun,
As radish roots declare, "We're fun!"
The sunflowers twist, trying to peek,
While crows quip jokes that trample the meek.

A worm recites its wiggly rhyme,
"I'm just working, not wasting time!"
The daisies chuckle, heads held high,
"Who knew dirt could make us fly?"

Chuckle with the herbs, so spry,
They argue who's the best to fry.
In this patch, absurd and sweet,
The roots' rhapsody is quite a treat.

Echoing the Seasons

Winter whispers, "I'm still fresh!"
While snowdrops poke through icy mesh.
Spring wakes up with a silly grin,
And giggles soft where life begins.

Summer struts in loud and proud,
With zinnias swaying in a crowd.
"Look at us, all bright and bold!"
While lazy bees around them scrolled.

Autumn drops leaves like jokes to share,
The pumpkins wink in orange wear.
With every change, a chuckle glows,
In nature's play, the humor flows.

Each season tosses wit around,
From blooms to frost, the laughs resound.
In every phase, the echoes tease,
Life's a giggle with playful ease.

Palette of Pleasantries

In the hues of red and bright lavender,
The daisies laugh, as if in slander.
"Have you seen that shrub in the back?"
"It's wearing purple... what a knack!"

A touch of green with herbs in tow,
Claiming they're the best in the show.
But marigolds shout with all their might,
"Why just look? We're a pure delight!"

The roses pout, "We're posh, you know!"
While violets wink, "We're a growing show!"
And tulips, proud, sway to the beat,
Making fun of those stuck in their seat.

In this color war of laughs galore,
Each petal pranks and wants some more.
The palette of pleasantries spins with glee,
As flowers frolic, wild and free.

Notes from the Nectar

Bees buzz by with a secret sound,
Whispering nectar is where joy's found.
"Did you taste that bloom? It's quite divine!"
While butterflies laugh in a swirl of line.

"I'll sip and dip, oh what a game!"
Said the bumblebee, lost in fame.
While ladybugs join in the fun,
"More nectar, please—oh, you're not done?"

The flowers beckon with scents so sweet,
"Try us now, we're the best to eat!"
While ants march by, in a frenzy to dine,
With crumbs of laughter, they stand in line.

Each drop of joy, a giggle shared,
In the buzzing world where no one's scared.
Notes from the nectar, silly and bright,
Remind us all, life's a sweet delight.

Ballad of the Butterflies

Butterflies dance, with wings so bright,
They sip on nectar, what a delight!
But on a daisy, they lose their grip,
And do a soft crash, a floral trip.

In sunlit fields, they twirl and glide,
Each with a secret they cannot hide.
They cheer the flowers, with silly cheer,
While bees just buzz, and roll their eyes here.

A moth once joined, thinking he's cool,
But flopped on a bloom, looking a fool.
The butterflies laughed, "You've got no flair!"
"That's okay," he said, "I'm free as air!"

And so they flit, through skies so blue,
Creating a mess, like kids in a zoo.
With every blunder, a giggle rings,
In their funny world of colorful flings.

The Enchanted Grove

In the grove where the critters play,
A squirrel named Fred just stole a bouquet.
He wore it proudly, a floral crown,
Until a bird laughed and knocked him down.

The trees whispered secrets, a rustling breeze,
While rabbits played tag right below their knees.
"Oh dear," said the owl, "it's quite a scene!"
With giggles from bunnies, it's a lively green.

A hedgehog once wished to impress a new friend,
But tripped on a root, and there met his end.
He rolled and he tumbled with style and grace,
While critters all chuckled, "Oh, what a chase!"

As night cloaks the grove, strange sounds arise,
With fireflies dancing, lighting the skies.
Each creature abounds in laughter and cheer,
In this enchanted haven, joy is near.

Canvas of Fragrance

Once there was a flower, quite vivid and grand,
Who dreamt of being more than just a stand.
He painted his petals in colors so wild,
But bees just buzzed, "That's the style of a child!"

Next came a lily, all chic and serene,
Who faked a faint to steal the scene.
"Oh dear," she gasped, "I'm fading away!"
The daisies just giggled, "You'll be okay!"

The roses held parties, all spruced up in style,
And daisies wore hats, just to add to the guile.
But one party crasher, the dandelion bold,
Gave everyone fluff, and the chaos unfolds.

With laughter and scent, the flowers unite,
Creating a ruckus, oh what a sight!
On this canvas of fragrances, colors entwine,
In the garden of giggles, where all is divine.

Verses from the Verdant

In the verdant fields, the grass has a laugh,
With daisies discussing their latest gaff.
"Did you hear about Joe, who grew really tall?
He tripped on a snail, and oh! Did he sprawl!"

The sunflowers chuckled, heads held so high,
While whispering tales as the clouds drift by.
"Once we danced with the breeze, oh what a sight!
Till we twisted our stems and took flight that night!"

A rabbit hopped in, with ears flopped about,
"Did you all hear? The wind blew me out!"
He fell in a patch of wild clover and laughed,
"Sometimes being silly is the best way to graft!"

So in leafy realms where hilarity reigns,
Every creature finds joy with all its refrains.
In verses of green, where laughter's a gift,
Life's a whimsical dance, in each spry little drift.

www.ingramcontent.com/pod-product-compliance
Lightning Source LLC
Chambersburg PA
CBHW071815160426
43209CB00003B/96